HOW TO
YOUR H

by
Chaya Srivastav

JAICO PUBLISHING HOUSE
Mumbai • Delhi • Bangalore • Kolkata
Hyderabad • Chennai • Ahmedabad

© Chaya Srivastav

No part of this book may be produced or utilized in any form or by any means, electronic or mechanical including photocopying, recording or by any information storage and retrieval system, without permission in writing from the publishers.

How To Manage Your Husband
ISBN 81-7224-218-2

Fifth Jaico Impression : 2003

Published by
Jaico Publishing House
121, Mahatma Gandhi Road,
Mumbai - 400 023

Printed by
R. N. Kothari
Sanman & Co.
113, Shivshakti Ind. Estate,
Marol Naka, Andheri (E),
Mumbai - 400 059.

TO MY HUSBAND
(who has let me manage him!)

JAICO PUBLISHING HOUSE

A Profile

Jaico Publishing House is one of India's largest publishing companies. Founded over fifty-five years ago, it takes pride in having published over 1,500 titles in a diverse range of subjects including Indian Literature, History, Politics, Sociology, Religion, Philosophy, Law, Health And Self-improvement. In addition, Jaico is a leading publisher of professional books and textbooks in Management, Engineering and Technology.

Mr. Jaman Shah, our late founder, established Jaico in 1946 as a book distribution company. Sensing that independence was around the corner, he aptly named his company JAICO ("Jai" means victory in Hindi). In tapping a significant demand for affordable books in a developing nation, Mr. Shah went on to initiate Jaico's own book publications. Jaico was india's first publisher of paperback books in the English language.

In addition to publishing its own titles, Jaico is a major distributor for leading U.S. and British publishers such as Mcgraw Hill, Simon & Schuster, Pearson, Addison Wesley, International Thomson And Butterworth Heinemann. The company has seven full fledged sales offices in Delhi, Kolkata, Chennai, Hyderabad, Bangalore, Ahmedabad and has its head office in Mumbai. Our sales team of over thirty individuals, direct mail order division, and website ensure that our books effectively reach all urban and rural parts of the country.

PREFACE

At the risk of incurring the wrath of women's libbers, I offer a formula for managing the husband. This is based on the philosophy that she manages others best who manages herself first! Despite all our claims to equality, we must accept the harsh truth that the failure or success of a marriage depends largely on the woman's capacity to compromise. Though seemingly loaded in favour of the husband, the solutions offered in this book are aimed at providing an alternative-another way of looking at problems. To that extent, I have fulfilled my commitment as a writer. The rest is upto the reader!

I'd like to acknowledge the help of Patricia Soanes, Shyam Trinath, Alakh Dalal, Mahesh Bharda and my sons Arjun and Anil.

HOW TO MANAGE YOUR HUSBAND
(if and when you get one!)

Statutory warning – Look before you leap ......
(exclusively for women)

Somethings don't change – like the four seasons, the sun... the moon... the stars... and the Indian husband! All husbands are alike but the Indian Husband is a breed apart. The wife however has changed over the years. This is where the problem begins! Most wives today imagine that getting a husband is what marriage is all about. But keeping him is surely more important! Most women do this by either being submissive and wretched or become bullies and cow down the spouse!

Neither is a satisfactory solution. What they need to perfect is the art of managing the husband without his realising he's being managed. This calls for a combination of tact, diplomacy, and shrewdness. Love and trust are naturally the foundation stones!

This little book gives you a practical approach to your Man Management! It may not guarantee a perfect husband but ensures a tension free atmosphere at home. All couples go through the same experiences and most of them have a common root cause – lack of understanding the spouse's point of view. Correct this and you have smooth sailing.

CHAPTER I

The honeymoon is over. The flowers have wilted, leaving only the fragrance behind (hopefully!). A change creeps into the relationship of man and wife. The atmosphere is charged with a subtle tension. Marriage has started withdrawing its magical mystery – its aura of other-worldliness. The fun and fancies are over and it's time to dig your heels in and get the marriage working. Perish the thought that once married, all you have to do is live each day through. You have to work like a beaver to build a happy nest!

Face reality:

The doting fiance has changed overnight to the disgruntled hubby! Remember – the shock must be equally great for him. He had never imagined that those petal soft cheeks of yours have to be nurtured by oily creams or your lovely tresses look like a crow's nest in the morning. Put yourself in his shoes and you'll realise why it pinches. But that's no reason why he has to holler for his towel or cup of tea! Surely he knows he looks so unromantic with stubbles and crumpled pyjamas!

The wrong way – howl back at him and throw abuses.
The right way – smile to yourself, march upto him with his towel, tweak his cheek and say 'lazy boy', lovingly.

The missing button
You never imagined that the gallant hero who helped you across gurgling streams and gently escorted you through crowded streets, could be so helpless with a needle and thread!

The wrong way – Tell him to sew his own button as you have to fix his breakfast.

The right way – Sew it for him as he munches his toast.

☐ *You don't become a slave if you mend his shirts or sew a button! It will take him sometime to get used to doing his own work – probably mama and sis did it for him! Fill in the void till you 'train' him to fend for himself!*

☐ ☐ *To avoid a crisis why not check his clothes a day earlier or after it's back from the laundry?*

☐ ☐ ☐ *Most men are spoilt by efficient mothers or get used to being sloppy, living in a hostel. Be patient till they are 'weaned' from this.*

And then – what's a mere button between husband and wife?!

Thinking of mama's pies
So, he remembers his mama often and slurps over the memory of her delicious sweets.

The wrong way – Call him a mama's boy and ask him to go back to her apron strings.
The right way – Agree with him. Before you set down the bowl of kheer say, "I wish it tastes like mama's kheer. I've tried to follow her recipe". He'll take a mouthful and say, 'perfect'.

The sister complex
He constantly thinks of his sister – how well she sings ... what a mischievous companion she was ... how he misses her prattle.

The wrong way – Say, "why didn't you marry someone like her?" with a sting.
The right way – Say, "I miss her too. She's great fun. Let's ask her to spend her summer holidays with us", – after all, if the brother you want to win, with the sister begin. She can be a very affectionate ally.

The relatives' convoy

A horde of aunts and sundry relatives descend on you periodically. Naturally, they are all his!

The wrong way – You complain bitterly to him and tell him you did not marry his entire dynasty.

The right way – Get so involved in being hospitable to the relatives that he finds it difficult to even get to talk to you! After a couple of such occasions, he'll be less enthusiastic about inviting them!

☐ *Remember. If your husband can stop being loyal to his mother and sisters, he can always do the same to you!*

☐ ☐ *The more gracefully you accept his people, the sooner will he accept yours.*

Don't think of it as an exercise in tolerance! Consider it an enriching experience! You will be meeting a whole new set of people who have formed the 'backdrop' for your husband's development as an individual. Don't be put off just because they are his people! You can always weed out those you don't 'vibe' with, gradually.

CHAPTER II

When two people have to live together day in and day out, there is bound to be a clash of interests. All this time, you have been having your way and he, his. Thrown together, you find yourself constantly up against situations which rouse conflicting reactions! This comes as a jolt because during the courting period, you have been on your best behaviour and willing to give in to the other's wishes, in a spirit of romantic sportsmanship! But marriage demands a continual 'best behaviour' which can be nerve wrecking! You have to perennially watch the weather chart for ....

His likes and your dislikes ....

He wants to sleep with the fan on, you don't like the monotonous whirr ....

The wrong way – Argue endlessly, fight, sleep in the other room or have your own way.

The right way – Get him to oil the fan to stop the whirring sound. Use a blanket if you can't bear the cold. When you are on different wave lengths on all such issues, discuss and come to a mutually satisfying arrangement in a calm frame of mind.

You plan to go out for dinner. He loves Continental food. You prefer Indian cuisine.

The wrong way – Insist on you having your wish or mildly give in to his ....

The right way – Have a good feed at home and opt for Continental, where you can have a dessert and the next time you go out, he will willingly take you to a restaurant of your choice.

Pulling the horse to the water ....
You want him to go with you for the ladies club annual dinner and he hates the idea ....

The wrong way – Keep saying how lucky Nina & Suman and others are as their husbands accompany them everywhere.

The right way – Tell him how eager the ladies club members are to meet him, especially after Nina told them how handsome he is (a few white lies permitted).

CHAPTER III

Getting hubby to pull his weight around is a Herculean task! There are some who have a natural flair for pottering in the house and setting things right. If you are lucky to have 'noticed' one such, appreciate him. If you are one of those hapless ones who's husband likes to laze around, putting things off for the morrow, burying himself in the newspaper, content to while away precious hours, while you have to battle with nitty gritty problems, then ....

Handling the handyman ....

The kitchen tap is leaking .... the store-room bulb needs to be changed .... the sideboard needs a fresh coat of paint ....

The wrong way – Nag him day and night about these. Tell him how useful Nina's husband is.

The right way – Don't talk about the problems to him. Instead, tell him how Nina complains about her husband who is totally useless. Give him instances of Suman having to run to her brother for odd jobs at home or Bela having to spend a lot on plumbers and carpenters for little repairs. After a day or two of this, casually mention the tap or bulb and wonder whom to call to set them right. Hubby will jump into action just to prove he's better than most!

Coaxing the reluctant Chef
You want him to help in the kitchen while he's averse to the idea.

The wrong way – Bang the pots and pans like a martyr and grouch at the dining table.

The right way – Serve a passable fare till he starts missing delicacies and asks for them. Sweetly tell him how tired you feel in the kitchen, managing on your own and suggest you have a cook. Remember to let your cooking get steadily worse and remember to keep your cool when he grumbles.

Remember – you are helpless!

Filling in for the maid
As usual, the maid stays away, leaving you to cope with the chores while hubby relaxes with the newspaper.

The wrong way – Bitterly complain about the maid, loudly envy men who don't give a damn and raise dust.

The right way – Switch on the music and combine calisthenics with sweeping and swabbing. Get so involved that his breakfast is delayed. Sweetly apologise for not going out with him in the evening and immerse yourself in soiled clothes and dirty dishes. Don't be surprised if he casually takes over dusting and other light chores!

☐ *Forcing your man to help in the house, only puts him off. What you need is tact. Without throwing tantrums, in a perfectly placid way, go about doing all the housework and at the end of the day, 'plonk' on the bed, exhausted – and fall asleep. Gradually, things will change – for the better! If nothing – you will lose those extra calories!!*

CHAPTER IV

Many marriages start cracking up for trivial and baseless reasons – like suspicion! This can start in an innocuous way and spread its tentacles quite viciously. Mutual trust is the answer to this and a free and frank confession of one's past. It's better to tell the spouse of one's past flames and affairs, so that the air is cleared and no third person can try to create mischief by giving a coloured version. Both must be immune to the insinuations of mischief makers.

Rout jealousy ......
He admires his colleague's wife and her hospitality on returning after a dinner at their place.

The wrong way – Say, 'I always knew you had a soft corner for her,' and turn away from him and pretend to sleep.

The right way – Join in the appreciation. Wish you were also like her. Say how lucky her husband is to have married her.

He has to interact with many women in his profession. Often, he has to dine or lunch alone with them.

The wrong way – Insinuate how he must be enjoying himself. Snoop on him by asking probing questions. Presume he must be having more than a business relationship with them. Go through his mail or coat pockets in search of evidence.

The right way – Trust him. Simpler said than done! Invite the women home for dinner. Befriend them and get to know their work. Be sympathetic about their work hassles.

You walk into his cabin in the office and find his Secretary on his lap .....

The wrong way – Make a scene. Abuse her, shout at him, break down and cry and threaten to divorce.

The right way – Pretend not to have noticed anything unusual. Finish the business you had come for and make a dignified exit. Later, call the secretary and tell her politely, not to mix business with pleasure. Don't confront hubby. Blissfully ignore the episode. Chances are he won't repeat it!

He has a roving eye and his feet willingly follow –

The wrong way – Rave and rant about his infidelity. Throw hints about divorce and alimony.

The right way – Assess the merits of the women in his life. Take stock of your own shortcomings. Work on yourself and rein him in by giving him what he wants. Occasionally, let him wonder whom you were with when you weren't at home! Let him get the feeling that you just might fancy a 'rove' too! Mind you – be very subtle or it will boomerang!

☐ *Remember, the forbidden fruit has more of an appeal than the easily available! The more you suspect him the more dangerously he'll like to live! Let him have his odd fling – just in passing, tell him how your friend walked out on her marriage to a philandering husband – let him put that in his pipe and puff away .....*

CHAPTER V

Compatibility in tastes and shared pastimes can cement a marriage. It's no mean achievement for two thinking individuals with diverse tastes to go through life without friction. Moonlight and roses soon lose their charm and you have to depend on less ethereal props to keep his interest. It's sensible to team up with a partner who has similar or almost similar likes and dislikes. But if you have forgotten the statutory warning, it's time for a bit of effort ....

Sharing pastimes ......
He loves watching sports events. He's crazy about cricket scores and engrossed in sports magazines.

The wrong way – March up to the TV and switch it off while he's watching a football game. Keep reciting local gossip when he's listening to the commentary or reading.

The right way – Show a keen interest in the proceedings and start enjoying it with him. Try and catch up on your own reading or sewing when he's immersed in the game and you are bored.

The same wavelength ....
He likes to discuss current events and politics.

The wrong way – Talk frivolously and switch on to local gossip.

The right way – Read up on the subject. Besides being able to hold his attention, you will improve your own knowledge. If you don't have the patience to read, ask him to explain to you what's happening.

Vibing well ....
He is all excited about his projects, however way out –

The wrong way – Throw cold water on the idea and taunt his wild imagination.

The right way – Go along with him – involve yourself – who knows, it might not be all that wild after all! He needs moral support and who better than his better half?!

☐ *As you have to live together, it's so much more fun to share each other's interests. If you encourage his hobbies, he will automatically encourage you in yours. This way, both will have developed an extra facet to the personality. If you make an attempt to learn and play bridge which he enjoys, he'll certainly respond by going with you to a play or concert which you enjoy: he wins – you win – both win!*

CHAPTER VI

What is marriage without quarrels? A couple who doesn't fight misses out on the spicy side. A good, wholesome quarrel session gets the pent up emotions out and purges you of all animosity. Most often, discensions are triggered by minor skirmishes. They can assume gigantic proportions or just fizzle out – depending on what you make of them. How sensibly you can quarrel and come out unscathed will be the test of your maturity and communication skills!

The blue moods
He has had a bad day at office and when he comes home, things get worse as he sees the damage caused to his scooter by the neighbourhood menace.

The wrong way – Call him unreasonable for venting his spleen on poor, innocent you who has had enough to cope with.

The right way – Give him a soothing cup of tea, bring out his favourite snack, talk of pleasant things that happened during the day

The heated discussion
In the course of conversation, he hints at some foible of your father or mother –

The wrong way –Unearth skeletons from his family cupboard brandish the eccentricities of his entire lineage.

The right way –Laugh the moment away. Later when you are in a better frame of mind and the atmosphere is congenial, let him know nicely how upset you are. Chances are he'll apologise.

Avoid 'I told you so' ......

These are 4 dangerous words. When you set out for a party, you suggest he fills in gasoline. He decides not to and drives on. On your return, the car stops! There's no gasoline.

JUST OUR BAD LUCK, HONEY! WE'LL TAKE A TAXI HOME.

I SHOULD'VE LISTENED TO HER WHEN SHE SAID...

The wrong way – Remind him of his folly in not heeding your advice.

The right way – Suggest he parks the car near the kerb, lock it and take a cab home.

☐ *He must be mentally kicking himself without your rubbing it in. Triumph over his discomfiture should not give you pleasure.*

Keep out trespassers ……

You have had a massive tiff with hubby. You want to unburden your pent up feeling, you want to complain about his behaviour –

The wrong way – Ring up your friend and pour out your woes. She will sympathise with you and agree that your husband is a monster. You feel better.

The right way – Sit down and write a stinker to him. Call him names and write all that you would like to say about him. When you are done, read it and tear it to pieces. You'll feel better!

☐ *Don't let a third person however close, enter your quarrel. Be like the proverbial pair of scissors – going in different directions but cutting anything that comes between.*

Making up gracefully

You are both feeling miserable about the quarrel you had last night. You both want to apologise but your ego comes in the way.

The wrong way – Keep waiting for him to extend the olive branch .... your wait is endless....go on!

The right way – Slip in a little note under his wallet. Say something romantic in it. He will see it just as he is about to leave for work and picks up his wallet. Watch the smile in his eyes. All's well!

☐ *Introduce silly but affectionate gestures into your life. Keeps you young. Slip in a love poem into his diary. When he goes to the office, he will see it first thing. Don't be surprised if he comes earlier than usual! Think of new and fresh surprises each time:*

☐ ☐ *Don't sleep over a quarrel. Try and make up by the end of the day. Make it a point to usher in and see off each day with a kiss!*

☐ ☐ ☐ *When alone, think of the situation objectively and apportion blame justly. Then, if you are at fault, apologise. If he's at fault, reason with him and tell him how the whole thing has been a result of misunderstanding. Don't accuse him of his wrong doing. That will only ignite a dying ember! After his own introspection, he'd have also realised his fault. The exercise is not to blame each other. It is to retrieve the situation.*

CHAPTER VII

Pride has no place in a marriage. And, why – should – I – when – he – doesn't attitude, does not get you anywhere. This does not mean slashing at one's self respect to keep the marriage going. It also does not mean lowering your defences all the time, to please hubby. But it means having a realistic approach to the situation. It means being broadminded and gracious about giving in, if it does not clash with your convictions. A man's ego, is more fragile – easily shattered – than a woman's. Saying sorry isn't as devastating to a woman as to a man. So, be more patient and tolerant ......

Entertain his ego
Anything you can do, I can do better, is his challenge to you.

> DON'T ARGUE WITH ME! NOTHING IS IMPOSSIBLE FOR ME. ANYTHING YOU DO I CAN DO **BETTER!**

> OF COURSE I KNOW IT, DARLING! YOU ARE A SUPER HUBBY!

> WHAT!? HAS SHE ALREADY FORGOTTEN HOW HE BURNT HIS FINGERS MAKING COFFEE..AND....

The wrong way – Pick up the cue and dare him to do this or that and see him lose.
The right way – Concede victory to him. Call him the best. Avoid situations where you have to compete with each other.

You have a better job than him and are earning a bigger salary.

WHAT IF I AM A BIT LATE? DON'T FORGET, I HOLD A MORE IMPORTANT POSITION THAN YOUR TWO-PENNY DESK JOB...

The wrong way – Remind him of this whenever you get an opportunity.

The right way – Don't make an issue of it. Neither flaunt it nor discuss it. If he grudgingly refers to it laugh it off as unimportant.

In social gatherings, you are more popular than him.

WHY DO YOU HAVE TO BE SUCH A BORE? WHY CAN'T YOU CIRCULATE LIKE ME?

The wrong way – Look triumphant. Talk about the way everyone fawned on you.

The right way – Draw him into your circle and make him feel part of it. If he is shy, try not to drag him into a boisterous crowd, instead choose to chat with people he is likely to be comfortable with and then slip out and circulate on your own.

Your parents are better off than his and live in luxury.

The wrong way – Make sure you spend all your holidays in the affluent abode of your parents.

The right way – Remember, his parents, however poor, are as important to him as yours are to you – so strike a balance. Spend equal time with both.

His friends are not too polished and you find them a bore.

> I DON'T FEEL LIKE IT, DEAR... WHY DON'T YOU HAVE A STAG PARTY WHILE I GO SHOPPING?

> OKAY, IF THAT'S THE WAY YOU WANT IT.

The wrong way – Shun them. Prevent him from mixing with them.

The right way – It takes all sorts to make the world – learn to accept this truth. Let him have a boys get together if you don't want to mix. But try and be gracious about it.

☐ *You are not in the game to be 'one up'. When you enter the fray, you are in it together – for the fun of it .... for togetherness – not to compete or be adversaries.*

Love is.... **having no ego hassles.**

CHAPTER VIII

Some men love to fill all their time with work. It could be a genuine case where work pressures are demanding – it could be indifference to family. Whatever the reason, many wives are forced to accept this habit of their husband's. Obviously, social life suffers, loneliness for the wife is inevitable and children become used to a one parent household. There is no point in getting worked up about this. The answer lies in finding options other than brooding or nagging!

Keeping his first love at bay ....
He keeps late hours at office. He brings home files and is forever at the telephone. He is wedded to his work and you have a grave adversary –

The wrong way – Accuse him of neglecting you. Keep grumbling while he is trying to concentrate on his file. Play loud music so that he cannot work. Keep ringing him up at the office to find out when he'll come ....

The right way – Accept the situation and find a way to make him acknowledge your presence – be absent. Try and do the vanishing trick a couple of times by going over to a relative's or friend's house. Let him wonder where you are – worry also. It will do him good to get anxious about your whereabouts. Soon, you'll find him coming home earlier! Let him work on his files at home. You take to reading or sewing at the same time. Don't make your presence felt. Gradually, you'll find his interest in files, decreasing.

Feeding the office fraternity
He has this horrible habit of bringing home his cronies for lunch with no notice.

The wrong way – Look stormy and frown throughout lunch, Make it obvious that you aren't too excited about playing hostess.

The right way – Be prepared for such contingencies! Stock your fridge with instant foods and ready masalas. Join a tailoring or flower arrangement class so that you are out during lunch time and give him a good packed lunch to ensure he stays in the office!

Putting up with his Boss
He has Boss fixation and wants to keep inviting him on and off for drinks or dinner.

The wrong way – Refuse to play hostess. Tell him to take the Boss to a hotel and feed him there.

The right way – Tell him later how Boss tried to play footsie with you at the dining table (repeat – white lies permitted) and made whispered advances during the evening! Drop gentle hints about your own partiality for the Boss's smile and charm.

Talking shop in parties
He has a tendency to home towards his cronies and discuss office affairs while you stand around bored.

The wrong way – Keep tugging at his sleeve and whispering loudly asking him to move on.
The right way – Wait for a break in the conversation and introduce a subject which will divert every one's attention – naturally it should be a topic of general interest and not controversial!

The touring spouse
He is away on tours very often, leaving you alone.

The wrong way – Pull a long face each time he comes back and give him a list of catastrophes that took place in his absence, like the leaking tap or dripping shower.

The right way – Find something useful to do while he is away – take a course or learn music. Make the home a warm and pleasant place when he comes back.

☐ *The quality of time you spend together is more important than quantity.*

☐ ☐ *If he prefers office to home, it does not mean he is wedded to his work – it means his home life is not as attractive as it ought to be. Take care!*

His job involves a lot of socialising and often he has to call off a date with you to fit in an unexpected business dinner.

The wrong way – Wait for him to get back, pull a long face, refuse to talk to him.

The right way – Supress your disappointment. Ask him pleasantly how successful was his meeting.

He likes to have a drink with his cronies occasionally.

The wrong way – Give him a menacing look and a deadline to be back home.
The right way – Let him go – better still, join him. You can sip a juice if you don't like alcohol.

☐ *Most wives cling on to the husband and have a dog-in-the-manger attitude. If you don't enjoy what he does, let him be. Being possessive drives him further away.*

☐ ☐ *A possessive attitude comes out of a sense of insecurity. Get over this by building up your personality. If he is ashamed to take you out for official parties, do something about yourself. Seek the advice of a friend and spruce up your speech, deportment, dress – try and be a person he will proudly show-off.*

☐ *If you are the type to watch the clock while he's away at work, obviously you are bored. The more you nag him, the longer he'll stay away. So, fill in your time with some hobbies. Develop a circle of friends or relatives you can spend time with.*

☐ ☐ *Stifling each other's individuality is detrimental to married life. A little isolation from each other is good occasionally.*

The upwardly mobile professsional
He is ambitious, go-getting, aiming at the stars. This means a hectic professional schedule and less of family life.

The wrong way – Be a constant thorn in his side. Demand his attention, keep calling him at the office. Accuse him of his neglect, decry his success.

The right way – Give him the moral support. Revel in his achievements. Be his alter ego.

☐ *For some men, their success is very vital to their well-being. Deprive them of this and you have a problem. Better learn to be proud of him and enjoy the fruits gracefully! As the wife of a successful man, you have many avenues to tap, so go ahead and use them.*

☐ ☐ *Look at the brighter side of it – There will come a time when he will have his fill of triumph. The important thing is to share his glory with him. Don't steal his great moments from him – be a part of them.*

CHAPTER IX

What seemed so 'cute' while courting might turn out to be an irritant when the euphoria wears off after marriage! That's the reality of living together – familiarity might just lead to contempt. Personal habits cannot be got over with easily and the less you push, the better. Naturally, you need not meekly accept all his misdemeanours in the name of 'habit'! It would, however, be worthwhile to assess your own foibles and remind yourself of the dictum, 'judge not that ye be judged'!

Coping with eccentricities
He loves percolated coffee and craves for the first sip at 6 a.m.

> HERE'S YOUR COFFEE, DEAR!
>
> OH! YOU ARE A DARLING!
>
> HI! CAN I HAVE MY BUSCUITS HERE?

The wrong way – Get up grudgingly and brew the stuff, plonk it on the bedside table and snuggle back into bed.

The right way – What you cannot cure – endure with a smile!! Anyway you are making it, do it happily (atleast pretend to be!) He will then willingly take on making the bed or securing the doors and windows at night.

☐ *One good deed attracts another!*

He is rather fond of smoking and you hate the smell of tobacco.

The wrong way – Nag him each time he lights a cigarette. Hide the matchbox – wet the cigarette.

The right way – Suggest he has a quiet smoke after dinner in the balcony while you clean up in the kitchen. Make a comfortable 'smoker's corner' for him in the house and tell him to use it whenever he smokes.

☐ *If averse to smoking, you should'nt have married a smoker at all! There's no way you can get anyone off smoking. The sooner you accept that with grace the less he'll smoke. Tension only drives him harder towards it!*

The sloppy spouse

He throws his things around, piles up clothes on the bed, misplaces handkerchiefs and is generally sloppy about his belongings.

The wrong way – Keep shouting at him.... ignore the mess.... criticise him before friends and relatives.

The right way – Clean up the mess. Don't sound or behave like a martyr. He will soon feel ashamed and improve.

☐ *Cleanliness and method is either inborn or acquired. It can't be forced.*

☐ ☐ *Don't go into marriage with the illusion that you'll reform a husband! Habits stay with a person so choose wisely. Remember the statutory warning.*

The short tempered grouch
He lets off steam at the slightest provocation. He raves and rants over trivial issues and doesn't spare you even in company.

The wrong way – Let off yours too. Match his hollering and get set for a verbal wrestling.

The right way – Shut up. Walk away. Let the steam evaporate. Avoid situations which are likely to trigger his volatile reactions. The angrier he gets, the calmer you stay and lesser you say.

The unromantic partner
He never remembers important milestones like birthdays and anniversaries. Doesn't even bring flowers and candy to cajole you. No compliments, no sweet nothings.

I'M GLAD THAT FITS YOU PERFECTLY, DARLING!... WHEN I SAW THAT COLOUR I COULDN'T RESIST BUYING IT FOR YOU...

ER, THANK YOU, DEAR!

SHE'S SO SWEET!... I SHALL REMEMBER HER BIRTHDAY THIS TIME, AND PRESENT HER S'THING GORGEOUS..

The wrong way – Compare him unfavourably to Nina's or Suman's husbands who are so loving and romantic.

The right way – Love him for his absent mindedness. Joke about his forgetfulness. Make up his shortcoming by being romantic yourself! Surprise him with little gifts and gestures and make him feel special. It will gradually rub off on him!

The Shylock...
He is tight fisted and getting money out of him is a Herculean task.

THIS SHOULD SERVE HIM RIGHT FOR BEING SO STINGY!

The wrong way – Be after him constantly .... steal from his wallet while he's bathing.

The right way – When you give him the household expenses hike up the amount. Build in a couple of rupees extra into each item – add a couple of things you may not need but can claim the money for.

☐ *Learn to manage finances cleverly – whether it's your own earnings or his. Money is the mischief maker in many broken marriages. Have the right attitude to it.*

... Sherlock syndrome
He is very possessive about you and keeps a watch on all your activities.

SO YOU WERE SPYING ON ME? WELL, I HAD A DATE WITH PRADEEP, MY BOYFRIEND OF COLLEGE DAYS

The wrong way – Call him a spy and goad him by giving him details of imaginary meetings with old flames

The right way – Allay his suspicions by boosting his confidence. Feed his ego .... tell him how important he is .... Keep away from people he'd rather you did not meet.

He loves to go to the Club in the evenings and booze at the Bar or play cards.

"YOU KNOW I GET BORED THERE, DEAR... BUT YOU GO RIGHT AHEAD. ONLY TRY NOT TO BE TOO LATE."

"OKAY, DARLING!"

The wrong way – Sulk and stay home. Don't warm his dinner when he gets back. Switch off all the lights and go to bed.

The right way – Even if you don't enjoy it, accompany him. You can go to the reading room or play indoor games. If you'd rather stay home, be graceful about it. Keep dinner in a food warmer and leave the night light on.

He loves to drink and forces you to keep him Company while you are averse to it.

> NO, DARLING...YOU KNOW HOW MUCH I HATE IT! I'LL SIP A SQUASH INSTEAD TO KEEP YOU COMPANY.

The wrong way – Cry and make a scene or meekly accept and drink.

The right way – You don't have to do anything you abhor. Be firm but polite. Agree to sip a squash. If he persists, ask him pleasantly to do something he dislikes to please you. He'll get the message!

He fancies swinging on the dance floor while you are self conscious.

WHAT DOES HE THINK HE'S DOING?! I'LL...I'LL TEACH HIM A LESSON!

The wrong way – Sit like a wall flower and steam within everytime he twirls a female partner in close embrace.

The right way – Shed your inhibition. Let yourself go. It is harmless fun and don't worry about what others may say! Who's life is it anyway?

A Health buff, he likes to jog early in the morning and insists on your joining him.

> WOW! I NEVER KNEW MORNINGS COULD BE SO BEAUTIFUL!

> THAT'S LIFE, DEAR! A WHOLE NEW WORLD IS OUT THERE... ONLY WAITING TO BE DISCOVERED...

The wrong way – Bury yourself deep under your blanket and pretend to be asleep.

The right way – Be a sport and put on your jogging shoes. A couple that jogs together stays together!

☐ *What seems like a dead end in marriage, can be turned to advantage. As long as it doesn't hurt you, there's nothing wrong in falling in with his 'idiosyncracies'!*

CHAPTER X

Many marriages sour due to a wrong attitude to sex. Quite often, both partners get into it with preconceived ideas drawn from books and films. Brought up in the conventional belief that sex is a 'taboo' subject to discuss, most women have qualms about this vital aspect of married life. It would indeed help matters if the woman has a frank chat with a lady Doctor, before marriage and get things in the proper perspective. Specialist advice is preferable because close friends may not have the expertise to tackle the subject effectively. There is of course, no universal code of behaviour in the intimacy of the bedroom. Each couple, will have to arrive at a mutually satisfactory equation of pleasure. Communication is the key to a successful sex life. It is wise to express fears, inhibitions and even pleasure, to the spouse. If you've had any traumatic experience before marriage, it's better to tell the spouse and win his/her confidence and sympathy.

It's your first night. You are left alone with him with the suggestive barbs of your friends ringing in your ears. He has definite designs of getting down to business while you'd rather not –

> JUST A MOMENT, DEAR... SHALL WE SIT BY THE WINDOW AND TALK FOR A WHILE ?...

The wrong way – Cringe into a corner. Shudder when he touches you. Pretend you have a headache. Think of mama and cry.

The right way – Buy time. Smile at him – talk to him about the excitement of the wedding. Divert his mind with anecdotes about the way your relatives or friends behaved. Draw him into conversation and gradually get his mind on to other things But also remember not to cheat him of his big 'night'!

The house is swarming with relatives staying back after the wedding. Your husband whispers to you to come for a tryst.

NO! I'VE GOT WORK INSIDE..! DO S'THING... WAIT FOR ME IN THE STUDY... BUT, REMEMBER... I'LL BE THERE ONLY FOR A MINUTE.

The wrong way – Hiss a refusal. Get busy with household chores to prove you're a dutiful daughter-in-law and keep out of his way.

The right way – Promise to be with him only for a few minutes. Create an opportunity for yourself to be alone with him. Even if you have your whole life before you, these stolen moments set the tempo for the future.

He is very selfish in his demands. Expects you to be 'willing' all the time.

CAN'T YOU THINK OF ANYTHING ELSE?

The wrong way – Snap back and refuse or look like a sheep in a slaughter house.

The right way – See the situation from his point of view! He finds you attractive and wants you! Don't blame him if you're so desirable!

You've had a gruelling day both at home and at work and want to curl up and die! He has other plans!

The wrong way – Vent your frustration at a crucial time. Call him names and accuse him of being self-centered.

The right way – Have a long leisurely bath. Spend a lot of time in the bathroom. Sprinkle yourself generously with powder. Slip into your clean fresh nightie. Hooh! You're not tired anymore and suddenly you have other plans too!!

He is a very clumsy lover and you are left to nurse your unfulfilled desires –

I DON'T WANT TO SOUND BRASH, BUT Y'KNOW, I TOO WANT TO ENJOY LOVE-MAKING...

The wrong way – Nurse a grouse too and refuse to cooperate or participate in lovemaking.

The right way – Let the moment pass. Later, when you are in a cooler frame of mind, tell him how you'd also like to enjoy lovemaking and express your desires.

Men are not aware that it takes longer for a woman to work herself up than a man and unless you communicate this at an appropriate time, your problem will continue!

You want romance, he wants sex. You want soft, tender, endearments he wants action –

> WHAT?! AT THIS TIME? YOU SHOULD BE ASHAMED OF YOURSELF... CAN'T YOU THINK OF ANYTHING ELSE?

The wrong way – Chide him for his one track mind and make him feel like a lecherous worm!

The right way – Create an atmosphere. Romance begins at breakfast and continues through the day. Wipe off that gooey cream from the face, look seductive. If he still wants only sex, that's the way he's made! But keep at it.

He likes acrobatics in the bedroom, you prefer conventional methods.

*IF YOU WANTED **ACROBATICS**, YOU SHOULD'VE MARRIED A **CIRCUS-PERFORMER!***

The wrong way – Stick to your preference and give him an 'or else ....' option.

The right way – Be adventurous for a change! The more you deny him something, the more he wants it, so be a sport and experiment!

He becomes the ardent lover boy in the early hours of the morning. You'd rather lie in peace and plan your day's schedule.

The wrong way – Push him away and reel off a list of better things you have to do!

The right way – Let him have his way. Then, you laze around, delay his breakfast – a couple of times of this and he'll not be so loving, so early in the morning!

☐ *If you have an incurable pervert for a husband, who likes to beat you up or force himself on you, you are indeed unfortunate. Many atrocities are committed behind the closed doors of the bedroom. But the normal, healthy husband with his normal physical urges, can be easily managed – with love and affection! If you deny him sex as a punishment – you're in for a worse one – he'll find it elsewhere. Sex is not the ultimate in marriage but it's very much a vital element in its success!*

CHAPTER XI

Marriage, in our society is not to an individual but to his whole family! He is such an integral part of a large group that any disharmony there, can throw its reflection on your married life. Indian men are still tied to their mother's emotional apron string. There is nothing distressing about this – on the other hand, it speaks highly of their loyalty to a person who has invested her time, affection and care in their welfare. The legendary mother-in-law feud continues, despite both women being educated and enlightened. In the tussle, the man has a difficult choice to make. This is where a wife can step in and smoothen relationships......

Coping with his family
Your mother-in-law has been particularly nasty to you, accusing you of enticing her son away from her.

> THAT'S ALL BECAUSE OF YOU! HE WASN'T LIKE THIS BEFORE MARRIAGE... HE WAS SO OBEDIENT AND...

The wrong way – Complain about her to your husband in the cosy intimacy of your bedroom.

The right way – Ignore the episode. Let ma-in-law vent her spleen and have her say.

Ma-in-law is all honey and sugar to you before hubby but bares her claws when he isn't around.

GO AHEAD AND WATCH THE MOVIE WITH HIM *BETI!* I'LL MAKE COFFEE FOR YOU TWO.

ER, THANK YOU, MOM!

WHAT A *NICE* AND UNDERSTANDING MOTHER I HAVE!

WHY CAN'T SHE EVER TELL HIM HOW TREACHEROUZ THE OL' LADY IZ?

The wrong way – Tell your husband how two faced his mother is.
The right way – Take the good with the bad, with a smile! No point trying to convince him about what he doesn't see!! Only turns him against you!

His mother loves to interfere in your life by dictating your behaviour.

The wrong way – Persuade hubby to cut himself off from the family.

The right way – Let her have her say but go ahead and do just what you believe in. Avoid altercations.

☐ *Though you have to take cognisance of his family, you have to mainly concern yourself with hubby. Turning him against them is not the solution as he's bound to resent it later. Tact and diplomacy are called for.*

☐ ☐ *As far as possible leave husband out of all the petty squabbles. If he gets to know of them, let it not be through you! Make light of all these pin-pricks and give trouble makers a wide margin.*

☐ ☐ ☐ *Men hate making a choice between family and wife. If your relationship with him is on sound and secure lines, you need not fear anyone else! So try and concentrate on cementing the husband/wife foundation.*

You are living in a joint family and your sisters-in-law cause mischief

I MUST TELL YOU WHAT BHABHIJI SAID TODAY:..

The wrong way – Wait for hubby to come home and serve him an endless list of complaints with tea.

The right way – Keep all this away from menfolk. They lose respect for you while they might sound sympathetic.

☐ *Let your husband discover for himself the petty mindedness of the family mischief makers. You must maintain a dignified neutrality which is bound to win him over. He has enough unpleasantness and politics in the office – spare him that at home.*

☐ ☐ *If other family members make it unpleasant for you, learn to become more assertive and develop your own defence mechanism. Don't try to lean on the emotional support of your husband. To satisfy you, he may console you, but deep within he will start blaming you.*

☐ ☐ ☐ *Peace and harmony can be achieved mainly by the large hearted acceptance of women in the family. Tolerance of the shortcomings of others, is a sign of maturity. Don't let family members drive a wedge between you and your husband. Keep them definitely out of your intimate life.*

CHAPTER XII

By and large, husbands are understanding and considerate. As long as they are looked after by the wives they don't go out of their way to create disharmony in married life. They are peace loving and want to think of home as a haven of love, after the tensions of work. It is very much upto the wife to provide the right atmosphere. The answer does not lie in submissive acceptance or passive tolerance. The essence of a working relationship is keeping your cool. The stronger of the two is invariably the calmer – this might be mistaken for docility but in this lies strength. When you are calm, you think better and therefore handle the situation to your advantage. But what happens when you marry a sadist – a brute?

Coping with brute force.....
Your husband is a regular boozer. He can't do without a daily swig.

> WAIT A MINUTE, DEAR! HERE'S S'THING TO GO WITH THAT POISON OF YOURS!

The wrong way – Grumble about his drinking habit everytime he pours himself a drink.

The right way – Let him drink in peace. Give him some nutritious eats. Create a peaceful atmosphere.

☐ *If you are averse to drinking habits, you should have followed the statutory warning!*

☐☐ *If he has become an addict over the years, you are partly to be blamed for not noticing the signs and nipping it early!*

Wife beating is his pastime.....

WELL, I'M NOT GOING TO PUT UP WITH YOUR SADISM ANYMORE. I'M WALKING OUT!

The wrong way – Get beaten and wallow in misery or make a public announcement and walk out.

The right way – Don't provoke the situation. When you see signs of his rising temper, quietly walk out of his presence and go to the bathroom.

He has a vile tongue and finds pleasure in abusing you.

The wrong way – Abuse him too. Brush up your vocabulary.
The right way – Find out the root cause. Most likely he has some frustration at work or is simmering over some childhood experiences. Bring him around with patience and love.

He's forever comparing you with other women and finding you wanting.

The wrong way – Compare him to other men unfavourably.

The right way – Make a mental note of these women and what he sees in them. Chances are it will open your eyes to your short-comings which you can overcome!

☐ *The point is to remember that you have no control over his action and words, but you can certainly work towards coping with it to your advantage.*

☐ ☐ *Men are spoilt brats at heart – apply the maternal technique of tolerance tinged with love and care.*

☐ ☐ ☐ *While you think you are making all the compromises and putting in all the effort, you are also scoring steadily over him! The sooner you realise this, the better you can manage hubby!*

Pampering

Children are on the scene and there is a storm brewing. He cannot see child crying and hates to be disturbed in the night when start mixing baby food.

> WELL, SHOUR BABY TOO I'M ALSO LOSING SLEEP BECAUSE HER!

The wrong way — Tell him it's his baby too and he jolly well put up with nappies and yells.

The right way — Shift baby to the next room and let him sleep in peace.

☐ It is tough to spend a sleepless night and go to work fresh and chirpy! You get maternity leave and you can make up your sleep during the day.

Sharing baby sitting
You want him to mind the kid while you iron.

The wrong way – Bully him into it by reminding him of his duty as a father.

The right way – Give him a choice – between ironing and baby sitting. If he chooses the former, you've nothing to complain. If he prefers the latter, it's his baby! Either way you win. N.B.: make sure you give him the choice in honeyed tones – in a way he cannot refuse. Cook him his favourite dish as a token of appreciation.

Baby or party

He wants to attend the dinner party at his friend's place. You can't go because of the baby.

> I HATE TO DISAPPOINT YOU, DEAR... BUT YOU KNOW, WE'LL HAVE TO PUT UP WITH IT. IT'S JUST A MATTER OF A COUPLE OF YEARS... ONCE THE BABY GROWS UP....

> OH! I WANTED YOU TO BE THERE FOR THE PARTY TODAY. BUT OKAY, IF YOU CAN'T MAKE IT...

The wrong way – Refuse outright to go with him. Tell him baby is more important than attending a party.

The right way – Explain how helpless baby is without you. Tell him how you'd love to come and all he needs to have is a couple of years' patience. Once the baby grows up, you'll go anywhere with him.

☐ *Remember – husbands are little boys at heart and find the presence of a child a threat to your affection for them.*

Draw in hubby into the baby-bringing-up activity. Let him feel part of it. Involve him not by dumping the little one on him as a duty but by letting him share the joys of a gurgle ....a toothless smile ....organise your schedules to give him more of your time by getting baby to sleep when he comes from work and wants your undivided attention.

The Papa's position
The little fellow says or does something wrong. Papa scolds him……gives him a whack.

The wrong way – Butt in and pull the child away…chide hubby for beating a mere kid.
The right way – Keep away. Let papa & son sort out the issue in their own way.

The little fellow complains to you about papa.

The wrong way – Take papa to task. Tell him not to be too harsh on the children.
The right way – Explain why papa had to do it and take up for him.

☐ *Don't keep punishments pending with a wait-till-papa-comes. Try & settle unpleasant happenings yourself. Leave papa to pet and play with the child. Don't paint him as the ogre who will come home from work annd swallow the naughty child. This only wins you cheap popularity from the child and drives father and child away from each other.*

Battling with home work
Your daughter brings home a pile of math problems and science questions.

The wrong way – Drag papa into it with a 'its' your business to teach the children.'

The right way – Express your helplessness, 'I just am not clever enough to cope with maths and science. Papa is more intelligent, go to him.'

☐ *The exercise is more fruitful if you motivate hubby to teach willingly. He will agree readily enough if you boost his ego (this can be used as panacea for almost all problems).*

Teenage trauma
The painful adolescent years are more difficult for your hubby to face than for you. He can't take the weird dresses, music and lifestyle in his stride.

The wrong way – Scold him for his outdated ideas. Ridicule his refusal to move with the times.
The right way – Be patient with his intolerance – explain that the teenagers' behaviour is a passing phase. Cushion the jolts by keeping the young people from getting into his hair!

The phone menace
Your son and daughter sit at the phone for long hours and hubby's temperature rises.

> I DON'T MIND YOUR TALKING OVER THE PHONE FOR HOURS, NOW. BUT WHEN DAD IS HERE, YOUR CALL SHOULD NOT EXCEED FIVE MINUTES. IS THAT CLEAR?

The wrong way – Call him an unreasonable man for coming in the way of children's pleasures.

The right way - Get the youngsters off the phone. Lay down the rule that no one continues a conversation for more than 5 minutes when dad's at home.

The fashion phobia
Hubby does not approve of your son's long hair and daughter's short dress.

The wrong way – Ignore his protests... tell him to be a sport.
The right way – Hear him out. Project his objections as your own and get the children to listen to you.

☐ *The position of a mother gives you the immunity from children's hostility. It's different with papa. So protect his image. Let him be the symbol of love and stability. You be the disciplinarian.*

CHAPTER XIV

The children are grown up and fly away. Daughter is married, son sets out seeking greener pastures. He is lonely and so are you.

> WOW! THAT SURE IS A FANTASTIC JOB YOU DID, DEAR.. WE'LL NOW HAVE A FINE GARDEN!

The wrong way – Look glum and shed copious tears. Accuse him of being hard hearted for not showing any sign of missing the children.

The right way – Be cheerful. He must be feeling lonely too, so keep him busy – visit close friends, go to shows, listen to music. Divert his attention.

Social Recluse
He prefers staying home and reminiscing about the children and talking about them.

The wrong way – Call him a sentimental fool.
The right way – Share his nostalgia. But remember the lighter moments so that you can laugh together and decrease the pain of separation.

CHAPTER XV

It comes at last! After years of sticking to a time bound routine, he is a master of his time and activities. All these years, he has put up with the whims of his colleagues and seniors, kept his cool, coped with professional tensions and brought home the bacon! The well deserved rest comes at last. Alongwith it also comes a feeling of restlessness. Only now, he realises how busy you are at home. He has nothing to do while you have your hands full – especially since he's at home now! He is more demanding – asking for a cup of tea at odd times, wanting you to go with him to the post office, expecting you to sit by his side and talk to him. Its upto you to make use of this opportunity to make your togetherness more meaningful.

Fighting boredom

Soon, boredom sets in. He starts missing work. He gets depressed. Wants to keep himself occupied but does not know how.

The wrong way – Blame him for not cultivating a hobby.
The right way – Involve him in your daily routine. Make him feel wanted…take to gardening and seek his help. Pass on lighter chores like shelling peas or picking rice and give him the feeling of being useful. Go out for long walks.

He dozes by the radio, reads a book, goes for a walk – generally lazes around while you sweat it out in the kitchen.

> WHAT HAVE YOU GOT IN THAT STUPID PAPER? YOU HAVE TO IDLE THERE WHILE I'M SLAVING IT OUT! CAN'T YOU TAKE UP SOME JOB?

The wrong way – Urge him to do something useful – take up a part-time job – make him realise how busy you are.

The right way – Enjoy togetherness. Tell him he deserves rest. Encourage him to savour each day leisurely.

You want to go for a religious discourse while he prefers a gossip session with old cronies.

THERE'S A PRAVACHAN BY THE SWAMIJI THIS EVENING... BETTER YOU GO THERE INSTEAD OF IDLING HERE...

The wrong way – Make him feel guilty about avoiding God! Tell him how necessary it is to resort to religion in old age.

The right way – Let him be. Religion is very personal. If he does not believe in it, there's no way you can force it on him.

☐ *Retirement is a traumatic experience. Ease it with understanding. Recapture the mood of younger days and relieve these halycon days.*

He has a habit of going off at a tangent on 'good old days' during a visit to friends or neighbours.

> I LIKE THE WAY YOU TELL YOUR STORIES OF THE PAST, DEAR... BUT THOSE YOUNG MEN ARE IMMATURE AND CAN'T UNDERSTAND YOUR VALUES..

The wrong way – Shut him up with a reprimand that no one is interested in his reminiscences.

The right way – When you are alone, gently tell him that other people might not be interested in his stories as they don't have his maturity and experience. Be a willing listener yourself.

Soothing the sick
Old age brings with it minor and major ailments. He is not too co-operative as a patient.

> DON'T YOU WORRY ABOUT ANYTHING, DEAR, I'M HERE TO TAKE CARE OF YOU..

The wrong way – Snap at him when he asks for water or a blanket or medicine.

The right way – Be sympathetic. Men are more fussy patients than women as they have lesser resistance. Accept this and indulge him – Pull your chair upto his bed and read or doze. Give him the feeling your are 'there'.

☐ *Men become more dependent on their wives as they grow older. The most aggressive male starts mellowing down. Women on the other hand have more tenacity and now more than ever, you should 'manage' your man – with kid gloves. The years of diplomatic treading are over. Now, its just living upto the faith he has in you. The child within which threw tantrums, misbehaved and troubled you all these years, becomes docile. From a wife you become mother. it's time to hold his hand and look into the horizon for the promise that lies beyond.*

**"GROW OLD ALONG WITH ME...
THE BEST IS YET TO BE....."**

SOME DO'S AND DON'TS TO REMEMBER ...

DO be frank about your previous love life, if you had any and 'tell all' to hubby.

DON'T expect too much from him.

DO share your thoughts and feelings with him and encourage him to do the same with you.

DON'T get upset when he points out an annoying habit of yours, which can be overcome for your own good!

DO be willing to make a change in your life if your married happiness depends on that.

DON'T expect him to agree with your beliefs, values and attitudes. Each to his own!

DO respect each other's privacy.

DON'T think you have to be aggressive to have your way –

DO remember that both of you have faults and shortcomings.

DON'T forget that when your marriage isn't going smooth, both of you are to be blamed.

DO have a sense of humour and laugh off daily pin-pricks.

DON'T – nurture grievances – have it out and sort it out.

DO keep a check on your words – they can hurt a relationship more than actions.

DON'T treat marriage as an institution – where you correct your husband!

DO look upon your hubby as a friend –

Marriage works out best when you are a wife with a mother's instinct. Mothers are tolerant, caring, loving, large-hearted, broadminded forgiving and indulgent. If you are all this, there's no way you can miss out on managing your husband. He is, inspite of all his macho tendencies, a little spoilt boy. Win him over and he'll be your slave for life!